Date

The Cherokee

Liz Sonneborn

Franklin Watts
A Division of Scholastic Inc.
New York • Toronto • London • Auckland • Sydney
Mexico City • New Delhi • Hong Kong
Danbury, Connecticut

Note to readers: Definitions for words in **bold** can be found in the Glossary at the back of this book.

Photographs ©2003: Art Resource, NY/National Portrait Gallery, Smithsonian Institution, Washington, DC, USA: 3 top, 29; Corbis Images: 48 (Bettmann), 45 (Medford Historical Society Collection), 46, 47; Hulton | Archive/Getty Images: 18, 19, 35; Mary Evans Picture Library: 20, 21; NASA: 4; National Geographic Image Collection: 39; nativestock.com/Marilyn "Angel" Wynn: 3 bottom, 8, 9, 10, 11, 12, 14, 24, 27, 28, 40, 41, 43, 51, 52, 53; North Wind Picture Archives: 31, 32; Oklahoma Historical Society/State Museum of History, #6393, Mariel H. White Collection: 37; The Overmountain Press: 22.

Cover illustration by Gary Overacre based on a photograph from Corbis Images by Peter Turnley.

Map by XNR Productions Inc.

Library of Congress Cataloging-in-Publication Data

Sonneborn, Liz.
    The Cherokee / by Liz Sonneborn.
        p. cm. — (Watts library)
    Includes bibliographical references and index.
    Contents: Origins—Meeting strangers—Learning new ways—Trail of Tears—A divided nation—The modern Cherokee.
    ISBN 0-531-12213-1 (lib. bdg.)   0-531-16245-1 (pbk.)
    1. Cherokee Indians—Juvenile literature. [1. Cherokee Indians. 2. Indians of North America.] I. Title. II. Series.
E99.C5S655 2003
975.004'9755—dc21

200300961

Contents

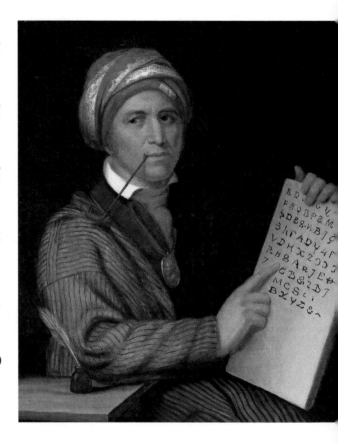

According to the Cherokee, Earth began as mud that grew into an island.

Chapter One

Origins

Long ago, plants and animals lived above the sky. But as their numbers grew, they became too crowded. Looking for a new place to live, Water Beetle dived into the water below the sky. When he came back to the surface, he brought up a small bit of mud. It grew and grew, until it became a great island. Today, we call that island Earth.

Buzzard next left the sky world and went to the mud island. The mud was not yet dry. When he lowered his wings, they sunk into it, forming valleys. When he raised them, they moved the moist mud upward, creating mountains.

After the mud dried, all the plants and animals went to live on the island. They were joined by Kana'ti and Selu, the first man and the first woman. Kana'ti and Selu became the ancestors of the **Ani-Yun-Wiya**, meaning "the principal people." The Ani-Yun-Wiya are now better known as the Cherokee.

The Principal People

This story is just one version of the Cherokee Indians' tale of how they came to be. As in the story, their traditional homeland was covered with river valleys and mountain ranges. Their large territory stretched over more than 40,000 square miles (104,000 square kilometers) in what is now the American Southeast. The Cherokee's original homeland spanned across eight present-day states: Virginia, West Virginia, Kentucky, Tennessee, Georgia, Alabama, North Carolina, and South Carolina.

By the 1500s, the Cherokee had a population of approximately twenty thousand. They lived in about fifty to one hundred large villages built along rivers. In the center of each Cherokee village was a plaza. There, people gathered to socialize and to perform religious ceremonies. Facing the plaza was a council house. People met in this large dome-shaped building to discuss important issues.

Villages also included houses where several extended families lived together. Their large rectangular houses were made from wood frames covered with cane, young sapling, or clay.

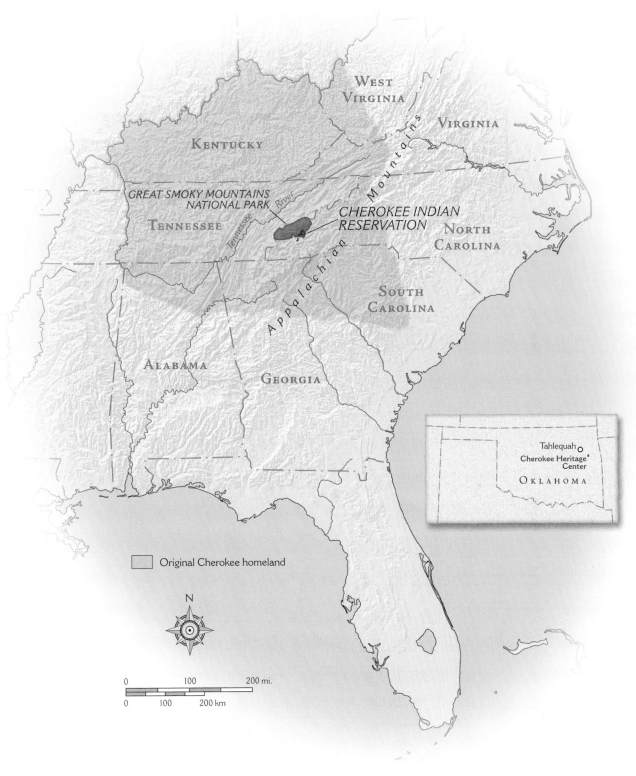

WEST
VIRGINIA

VIRGINIA

KENTUCKY

*GREAT SMOKY MOUNTAINS
NATIONAL PARK*

Tennessee River

CHEROKEE INDIAN
RESERVATION

TENNESSEE

NORTH
CAROLINA

SOUTH
CAROLINA

Appalachian Mountains

ALABAMA

GEORGIA

Tahlequah
Cherokee Heritage
Center

OKLAHOMA

Original Cherokee homeland

N

0   100   200 mi.

0   100   200 km

This photograph shows some traditional Cherokee buildings.

Most people in a household belonged to the same **clan**. Clan members believed they were descended from the same ancestor and considered themselves closely related. Among the Cherokee, children always belonged to the clan of their mother.

Gifts from the Earth

Each Cherokee household had a small private garden. However, most of the Cherokee's food was grown in large fields they farmed together. Although men sometimes cleared the land, women were responsible for planting, tending, and harvesting the crops. The women often looked after their children while they worked. Older children helped with the planting and weeding.

Cherokee women grew beans, squash, pumpkins, and sunflowers, but their most important crop was corn. Women cooked with dried corn, making tasty soups and stews with it. They also ground corn into a meal used to make cornbread. Women often flavored their bread batter with chestnuts. Other wild plant foods they gathered included berries, roots, crab apples, hickory nuts, and walnuts.

Men contributed to the Cherokee's food supply by fishing. They made spears, hooks, and traps to catch fish in their

Corn, beans, squash, and pumpkins were a part of the traditional Cherokee diet.

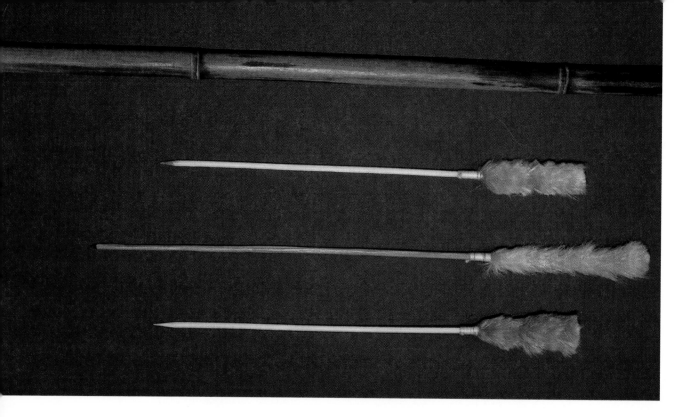

A Cherokee hunter might use a blowgun (top) and darts to catch his prey.

Hunting with Blowguns

Using a blowgun, a skilled hunter could shoot a dart as far as 60 feet (18.3 meters).

territory's many rivers and streams. Sometimes, they fished by blocking off a stream and adding ground horse chestnuts or walnut bark to the water. The ground nuts contained a natural poison that stunned fish but was harmless to humans. As the fish floated to the surface, Cherokee fishermen could simply scoop them up with their hands.

Cherokee men were also hunters. Using bows and arrows, they stalked large game, such as deer and bear. They also made blowguns from the stems of cane plants to hunt rabbits, turkeys, squirrels, and other small animals.

In addition to meat, animals provided the Cherokee with skins they used to make their clothing. In warm weather, men wore breechcloths and women wore skirts made of deerskin. In winter, they added fur capes and moccasins. Women sewed their families' clothing using bone needles. They also wove baskets from cane and bark strips and molded pottery from clay.

Leading the Tribe

The Cherokee were not ruled by a single leader. Instead, each village was governed by a council that met regularly to take over matters of local interest. Everyone in attendence had to agree on every decision made by the council.

Villages also had two chiefs. The white chief helped solve disputes and organize ceremonies and other events affecting

This is the inside of a Cherokee council house where the council would meet to discuss any issues.

These people are performing the Green Corn Dance.

the entire village. The red chief was in charge of making war preparations and leading parties of warriors into battle.

The Cherokee often fought with other Indians. They usually went to war to avenge the deaths of warriors killed in battle. During warfare, the Cherokee sometimes captured people from enemy tribes. Women and children taken captive were generally adopted into the tribe. Male captives were more often tortured and killed. Their fate was decided by **war**

women. These women were highly respected tribe members who accompanied war parties. They cooked the warriors' food and advised them about their battle strategy.

Before going to war, men performed ceremonies to ensure their success in battle. For several days, they purified their bodies by fasting and drinking a strong tea called **black drink**. Similar rituals were performed before games of stickball, a sport much like lacrosse. During these intense games, players were often injured. Because the sport was so violent, the Cherokee nicknamed it the "little brother of war."

The Cherokee also performed ceremonies to give thanks and keep their world in balance. The most important was the **Green Corn Ceremony**. It was held each summer when the corn crop ripened. During the ceremony, people cleaned their houses, threw away their old food stores, and put out the fire that burned in the council house. They built a new council fire and then held a great feast to celebrate the new year.

It is believed that the explorer Hernando de Soto visited the Cherokee in the 1500s.

Chapter Two

Meeting Strangers

In 1540, the Cherokee probably had their first encounter with non-Indians. They were Spaniards led by the explorer and adventurer Hernando de Soto. Wearing full armor in the hot sun, de Soto and his heavily armed men rode on horseback into the Southeast. With them were hundreds of Indians from other tribes. They had been enslaved by the Spaniards and forced to carry their supplies.

De Soto had come to the Southeast in search of gold. Other Spanish explorers had become rich by stealing the precious metal from Indian settlements farther south in present-day Mexico and South America. But to their disappointment, the Spaniards discovered that the Indians of the Southeast had no gold. De Soto's expedition soon left the region, taking with them many Indians as slaves.

Over the next hundred years, the Cherokee met few other non-Indians. Even so, their early contact with the Spanish had a huge impact on the Cherokee during this time. These outsiders introduced smallpox and the measles to the tribe. The Cherokee had never before been exposed to these European diseases, so they had no natural **immunities** to them. As a result, the Cherokee usually died after catching them. Due to disease, the tribal population dropped sharply.

Trading with Non-Indians

In the late 1600s, non-Indians again began to trickle into Cherokee territory. They were traders from colonies established by English settlers along the coast of the Atlantic Ocean. These Englishmen wanted to trade with the Cherokee for deerskins. The traders could make a healthy profit by shipping deerskins to England, where they were used to make leather goods.

English traders brought the Cherokee new goods that made their lives easier. These goods included cloth, pots, kettles, and metal tools. The traders had metal tools that were far more durable than the ones the Cherokee made themselves from stone and bone. The English also gave the Cherokee guns. With these weapons, the Cherokee could kill many more animals during a hunt. Guns also helped them win battles against their Indian enemies.

These new goods brought changes to Cherokee life. Not all of these changes were good. Over time, the tribespeople began using metal tools and weapons more and more. As a result, they became dependent on non-Indians for these necessities.

Trade with non-Indians also encouraged Cherokee men to hunt more than ever before. In the past, they had killed only enough animals to feed and clothe their families. Now, they spent much more time hunting in order to have enough skins to trade. The Cherokee were soon overhunting, endangering the animal population in their territory.

New Enemies

Another result of trade with non-Indians was increased warfare. Traditionally, the Cherokee went to war to avenge the deaths of warriors killed by other tribes. But, after becoming

The Deerskin Trade

In 1735 alone, Cherokee hunters traded more than one million deerskins to the English.

partners with non-Indian traders, some tribesmen began fighting for the sole purpose of taking captives. Cherokee warriors could become wealthy by trading the captives to the English. The traders then sent them to the English colonies. There, the captives were sold as slaves.

The Cherokee were also drawn into wars fought between the English and their enemies. In the early 1700s, for instance, three hundred Cherokee warriors helped the English drive the Tuscarora tribe out of lands claimed by the English in what is now North Carolina. More often, the English asked the Cherokee to help them fight the French. Throughout the early 1700s, the English and French battled for control of what is now the eastern United States and Canada.

This rivalry eventually led to the French and Indian War (1754–1763). The English gave the conflict this name because most Indian tribes sided with the French. The Cherokee, however, at first remained loyal to the English. George Washington, then a lieutenant colonel in the English army, called the Cherokee's assistance in the war "very necessary." But he also warned his fellow soldiers that, "One false step might not only lose us *that*, but even turn them against us."

The Cherokee agreed to help the English fight the French-allied Shawnee Indians. A severe winter storm, however, forced the war party to return home before the battle. On the way, starving Cherokee warriors slaughtered some unpenned cows belonging to English farmers. The farmers responded by killing several of their Cherokee allies. Angered by the

At first, the Cherokee sided with the English in the French and Indian War.

The Cherokee fought the English that were sent to their homeland in 1760.

murders, young Cherokee warriors began raiding English settlements.

A group of Cherokee leaders wanted to end the fighting. They traveled to Fort Prince George, an English fort in their territory, to negotiate a truce in 1759. Instead of talking with the Cherokee leaders, the English placed them in prison. Four

months later, Cherokee warriors stormed the fort. During the battle, the English killed the Cherokee imprisoned there.

Once allies, the Cherokee and English now became bitter enemies. About 1,600 English troops were sent to Cherokee territory in June 1760. The Cherokee, led by Oconostota, drove these soldiers from their lands. But an even larger English force returned the next summer. They defeated the Cherokee and wrecked many of their villages. The English also destroyed 1,500 acres (607.5 hectares) of farmland. Many Cherokee were left to starve.

The Revolutionary War

To make peace with the English, the Cherokee gave them much of their best hunting grounds. In 1775, they also lost territory in present-day Kentucky and Tennessee in an illegal land sale. A group of Cherokee led by Dragging Canoe objected to the sale. They grew angry as colonists began moving onto the land.

Despite their past troubles with the English, the Cherokee took their side in the Revolutionary War (1775–1783). During this war, colonists who called themselves Americans were fighting for their independence from England. Dragging

Nancy Ward

In 1755, the Cherokee went to war with the Creek tribe. A young woman named Nanye'hi accompanied her husband to the battlefield. Nanye'hi sang war songs to inspire the warriors. When an enemy's bullet struck her husband, she grabbed his gun and took his place in battle. Because of her bravery, Nanye'hi was given the title Beloved Woman—one of the highest honors a Cherokee could earn.

As a Beloved Woman, Nanye'hi had a great deal of influence over her people. She used her position to try to persuade the Cherokee to live in peace with the non-Indian settlers in their lands. Nanye'hi herself was briefly married to a white trader named Brian Ward. After this marriage, non-Indians called her Nancy Ward.

With the outbreak of the Revolutionary War, some Cherokee began fighting Americans in the region. Hoping to end the bloodshed, Ward warned non-Indians of attacks planned on their settlements. When the war ended, she helped negotiate the tribe's first treaty with the United States.

Canoe took advantage of the situation by attacking settlements of Americans who had moved onto the Cherokee's former territory. The Americans sent a force to fight the Cherokee. Already weakened by years of war, the Cherokee were again defeated.

The Americans won the war in 1783. By this time, the Cherokee were tired of fighting. In Hopewell, South Carolina, in 1785, they negotiated a peace **treaty** with the newly formed government of the United States. During the proceedings, Nancy Ward, a respected Cherokee elder, spoke for the tribe. She told the assembled leaders that, though she was old, she hoped to have more children because now they could grow up in peace.

Other people wanted to take the land away from the Cherokee because it was rich in natural resources.

Chapter Three

Learning New Ways

After the Revolutionary War, the Cherokee faced a new challenge. They were now surrounded by American settlers. Many were hostile to the Cherokee. They still thought of the Cherokee as their enemy. Some Americans also looked down on the Cherokee as inferior. They believed that whites, not Indians, deserved to have control over the Cherokee's rich land.

The "Civilization" Movement

Forced to adapt to their new situation, many Cherokee decided to change some of their ways. At the urging of the U.S. government, the Cherokee started adopting non-Indian customs and beliefs. Officials referred to this as "civilizing" the Cherokee. The new United States could not afford another war with the Cherokee and their Indian neighbors. By encouraging them to live like whites, U.S. officials hoped the Indians would peacefully become part of American society.

Non-Indian **missionaries** also encouraged the Cherokee to change their customs. Missionaries wanted the tribe to abandon its traditional ceremonies and convert to Christianity. Some tribal members did become Christians. Most, however, had little interest in the missionaries' religion, though the tribe did allow the missionaries to establish schools on tribal lands. Some Cherokee wanted their children to learn to speak, read, and write English so they could better communicate with non-Indians.

On their own, the Cherokee chose to change their government. In the past, no one person or group could speak for the entire tribe. But now the Cherokee needed a national government to deal with U.S. officials. They formed the General Council. It was made up of representatives elected from eight districts. The council chose one of its members to serve as the tribe's **principal chief**.

The new tribal government soon began putting its laws in writing. The tribe also began publishing the *Cherokee Phoenix*.

The General Council

The structure of the Cherokee's General Council was modeled after that of the U.S. Congress.

The newspaper printed local and world news in both Cherokee and English and was the first newspaper ever published in a Native American language.

This photograph shows an early issue of the Cherokee Phoenix.

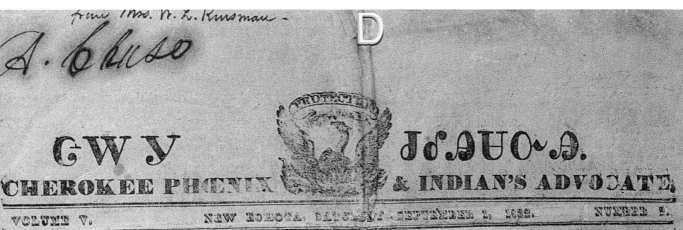

Preserving Tradition

As the Cherokee learned to blend old and new ways, many prospered. Some grew rich running plantations, or large farms worked by African-American slaves. For instance, John Ross, who served as principal chief from 1827 to 1866, owned nineteen slaves. He earned so much from his businesses, he could afford to live in an elegant home with imported furniture and china. Ross and several other Cherokee were among the wealthiest people in the American Southeast.

Still, some Cherokee were reluctant to embrace non-Indian ways. These **traditionalists** were happy with their traditional customs. Pressured to change by non-Indians and other Cherokee, some decided to live apart from the rest of the tribe. Settling along the Oconaluftee River, they became known as the Oconaluftee Band or Oconaluftee Cherokee. In 1819, they gave up their rights as Cherokee and became citizens of the United States.

Other traditionalists chose to leave their homeland altogether. They established new settlements first in what is now Arkansas and later in present-day Oklahoma. These western Cherokee, however,

Sequoyah and the Cherokee Written Language

Like most Indian tribes, the Cherokee traditionally had no system of writing down their spoken language. That changed in the early 1800s because of one brilliant Cherokee named Sequoyah.

For many years, Sequoyah worked alone in his cabin. Initially, he tried inventing a symbol for every Cherokee word. Finding this too complicated, he instead created a symbol for each sound in the Cherokee language.

Sequoyah first taught his writing system to his young daughter, Ahyokeh. She caught on quickly.

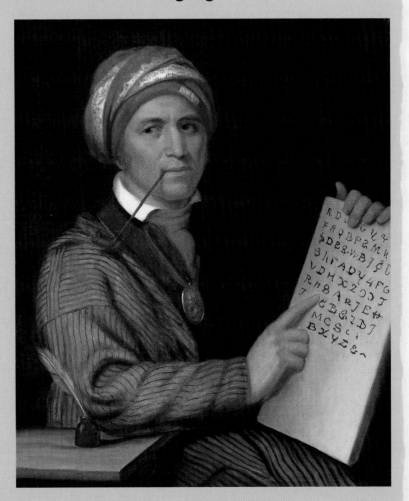

To introduce his invention to the tribe, he and Ahyokeh began holding public demonstrations. At these shows, Ahyokeh amazed the crowds by reading out loud messages written down by her father.

Sequoyah's writing system was an immediate success. With only a few lessons, any Cherokee could learn to read and write. Sequoyah's writing system meant that people could send letters to loved ones far away and read about important events in the tribe's newspaper. It also allowed the tribal government to write down its laws and constitution.

continued to have close ties with relatives who stayed behind in their old lands.

U.S. officials encouraged other Cherokee to move west as part of its **removal** policy. Beginning in the early 1800s, the United States made plans to move eastern Indians to an area west of the Mississippi River. The Indians' eastern lands could then be settled by non-Indian Americans.

The U.S. officials were particularly eager to see the Cherokee in Georgia leave for the West. In 1802, the United States had made an agreement with the state. In it, Georgia had agreed to give up land in what is now Alabama and Mississippi. In exchange, the United States had promised to move all Indians—including the Cherokee and the Creek—out of Georgia.

At the time, the U.S. government assumed it could persuade the Cherokee to move west voluntarily. But wealthy tribal leaders such as Ross had no desire to leave their homes and businesses. Less prosperous Cherokee were also determined to stay in their homeland. They believed the land had been made for their people. They saw no reason to leave the place where their ancestors had lived for centuries.

The Cherokee made their intentions clear in 1827. In that year, tribal leaders wrote a constitution. The document set out the precise boundaries of the Cherokee Nation, which then included lands claimed by Georgia, Alabama, Tennessee, and North Carolina. With the constitution, the tribal leaders declared to their white neighbors that, in their eyes, this territory belonged to no one but the Cherokee.

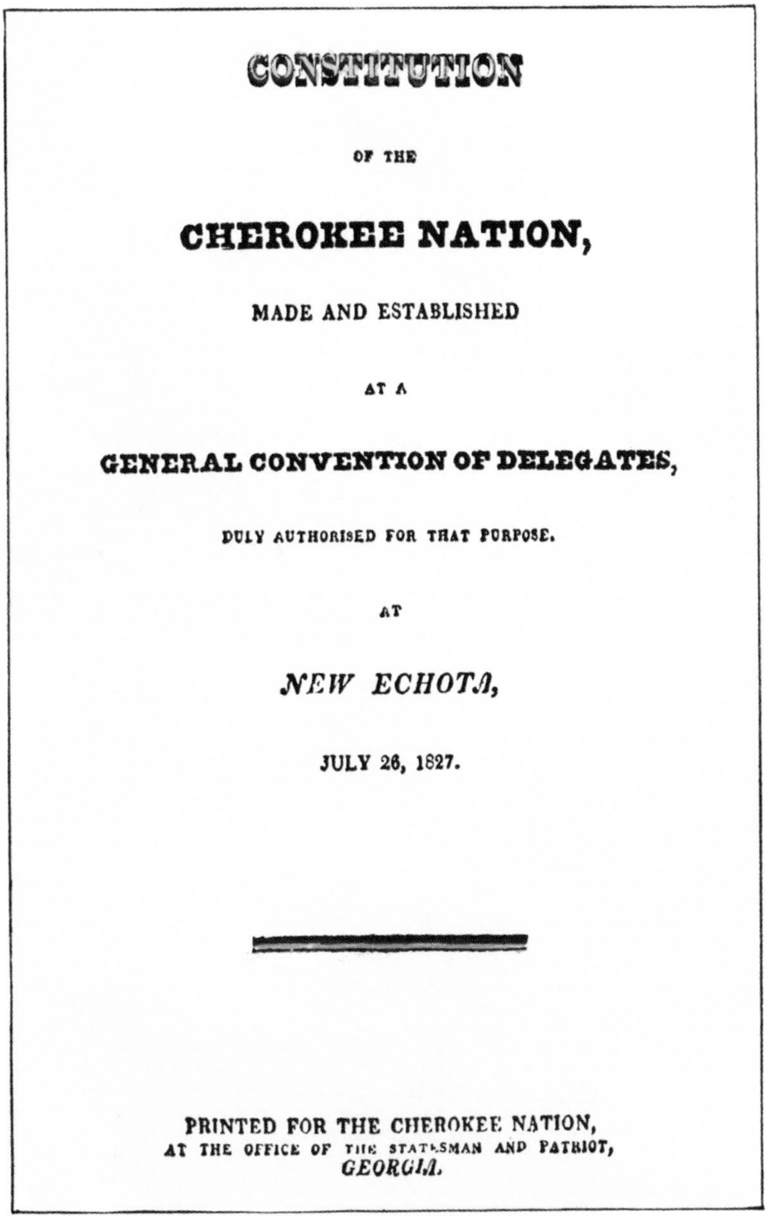

CONSTITUTION

OF THE

CHEROKEE NATION,

MADE AND ESTABLISHED

AT A

GENERAL CONVENTION OF DELEGATES,

DULY AUTHORISED FOR THAT PURPOSE.

AT

NEW ECHOTA,

JULY 26, 1827.

PRINTED FOR THE CHEROKEE NATION,
AT THE OFFICE OF THE STATESMAN AND PATRIOT,
GEORGIA.

In their constitution, the Cherokee outlined the boundaries of their homeland.

Once gold was discovered in Cherokee territory even more outsiders hungered to remove the Cherokee from their lands.

Chapter Four

Trail of Tears

In 1829, gold was found in Cherokee territory. The discovery excited land-hungry Americans in Georgia. More than ever they wanted to see all Cherokee Indians removed from the state. Then, they could take not only the Cherokee's lands but also their gold.

Decades before, the U.S. government had pledged to give non-Indians control over the Cherokee's territory in Georgia. With the discovery of gold, Georgians were no longer willing to wait for the government to make good on its promise. Instead, the state legislature decided to take matters into its own hands. It passed a series of laws designed to force the Cherokee to leave their lands and head west.

The Anti-Cherokee Laws

With its anti-Indian laws, Georgia stripped the Cherokee of all their rights. One law forbade the Cherokee from mining gold on their own land. Another declared it illegal for a Cherokee to testify in court. Still another made it a crime for a Cherokee to dissuade other tribe members from moving west.

The anti-Indian laws sent a message to non-Indians in Georgia. They could now do whatever they wanted to the Cherokee's land and property without fear of punishment. Some non-Indians burned Cherokee houses and destroyed their fields, leaving many tribe members homeless and hungry. Others freely stole from the Indians. In one instance, Principal Chief John Ross came home from a trip to Washington, D.C., to find that white settlers had taken over his house.

The Cherokee's situation grew even worse during Andrew Jackson's presidency. Jackson was a great supporter of the removal policy. In 1830, he pushed the Indian Removal Act through Congress. This law provided funds for negotiating removal treaties with the Cherokee and other tribes in the East.

Fighting Removal

As the pressure to move west grew, the Cherokee decided to fight back in court. In 1832, the tribe brought *Worcester v.*

Georgia before the U.S. Supreme Court. The court declared that Georgia law did not apply to the Cherokee people. The ruling, however, did nothing to stop the Georgians from taking over Cherokee property and land. The Georgians simply ignored the ruling, and President Jackson refused to enforce it.

Treaty negotiators continued to call for the Cherokee's removal, but John Ross could not reach an agreement with them. Leaders of other nearby tribes, however, such as the Creek, Choctaw, and Chickasaw, were persuaded to sign removal agreements. In some cases, the negotiators bought the leaders' support with bribes.

Some prominent Cherokee, including Major Ridge and Elias Boudinot, began to question Ross's leadership. They did not believe he could win the fight against removal. They were afraid that if the Cherokee did not sign a treaty soon, the United States would take everything they had. But these men believed, if the Cherokee acted now, they could at least negotiate a decent price for their land and not lose all of their possessions.

Major Ridge doubted that Ross could stop the removal of the Cherokee and worked with others to negotiate with the U.S. government directly.

By 1834, these men became known as the **Treaty Party**. They secretly began to negotiate with U.S. officials. The great majority of Cherokee, however, continued to support John Ross and to oppose removal.

The Treaty of New Echota

Despite the wishes of most Cherokee, several hundred Treaty Party members met with negotiators in December 1835. The party leaders signed the Treaty of New Echota. In it, they sold the Cherokee homeland for $5 million and agreed to move the tribe to **Indian Territory** (now Oklahoma).

Ross and most other Cherokee were furious when they found out what the Treaty Party had done. The tribe presented the U.S. government with a petition protesting the treaty. Many important non-Indian leaders agreed that the Cherokee were being cheated out of their land. Nevertheless, the Senate ratified, or approved, the New Echota treaty. The Cherokee were given two years to leave their homes.

After the treaty's ratification, hundreds of Treaty Party Cherokee began the trip west. The first group left in January 1837. They traveled in wagons filled with their personal possessions. During the trip, they were attended by African-American slaves. After a fairly comfortable journey, they arrived in their new lands just in time to plant their spring crops.

Most Cherokee, however, still held out hope that they would be allowed to stay in the East. They made no preparations to leave their homes. In May 1838, the deadline for their removal, more than seven thousand federal troops and volunteer soldiers arrived in the Cherokee Nation. A few Cherokee evaded the soldiers and fled into the mountains, but most were rounded up and placed in holding camps. They were not

A Disgraceful Treaty

Former president John Quincy Adams opposed the Cherokee's removal treaty, saying "it brings eternal disgrace upon the country."

allowed to take any of their belongings, which were quickly looted by white settlers. To ensure that the Cherokee could not escape and return home, soldiers burned many of their houses and fields.

The Oconaluftee Cherokee watched nervously as their kin were forced into the camps. Although they were legally citizens of the United States, they feared they could be next. Their situation grew even more desperate after an Oconaluftee named Tsali and his two sons killed two of the soldiers. The army demanded that the Oconaluftee help them catch Tsali. Fearing what might happen if they refused, they found Tsali's hideout and killed him.

The Journey West

In the spring of 1838, about 3,000 Cherokee were forced to travel to Indian Territory by land and water. Many suffered from hunger and disease, and several died. As summer

The Story of Tsali

Because of his willingness to stand up against Americans, Tsali became a folk hero among the Cherokee in the East.

This painting depicts the Cherokee during their relocation to the West.

approached, temperatures soared. Principal Chief Ross feared many more would die if the migrations continued. He convinced the government to postpone the Cherokee's removal until autumn.

The Cherokee remaining in the camps were forced to spend the sweltering summer locked in prisonlike stockades. They were fed little, and disease spread quickly through the camps. Their drinking water was dirty, and they had almost no water for bathing. Nearly as horrible as their physical suffering was the grief they felt. Their homes, their land, their old way of life—all were now gone. Thousands also lost their lives due to the terrible living conditions.

In August, the removal began again. Group after group of Cherokee started toward Indian Territory, mostly on foot. Their few wagons were used primarily to carry their small stores of food and supplies. The conditions on the trail were difficult, especially for the elderly and the ill. With little food and only the clothing on their backs, they were forced to

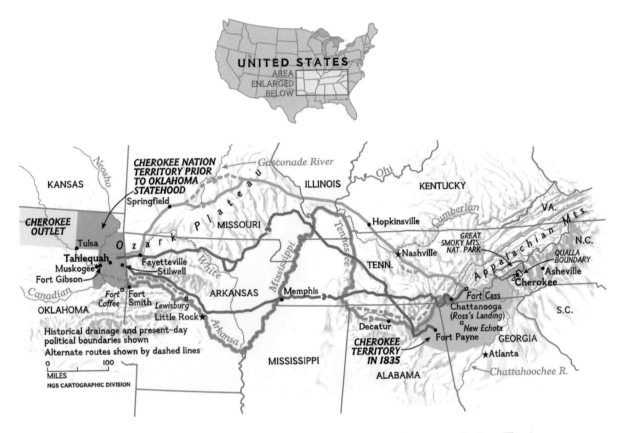

This map shows the many routes the Cherokee traveled to get to Indian Territory.

march through heavy rain and snow. The trail was soon paved with graves.

The Cherokee gave a name to their miserable journey to Indian Territory. They called it Nunna daul Tsunyi—the Trail where They Cried. The tragic event is now known as the **Trail of Tears**.

Death on the Trail

About one out of every four Cherokee died as a result of the removal.

The people who were able to stay in North Carolina became known as the Eastern Cherokee. This photograph shows part of the Cherokee's original homelands in the Great Smoky Mountains.

Chapter Five

A Divided Nation

The Trail of Tears left the Cherokee a divided people. The tribe members who managed to stay in North Carolina became known as the Eastern Cherokee. Those who settled in Indian Territory became known as the Western Cherokee.

The Cherokee of Indian Territory were further divided into several factions. As the survivors of the Trail of Tears struggled to build new lives, differences among these groups added to their troubles. In fact, within months of their arrival, the infighting among the Western Cherokee threatened to tear the tribe apart.

Cherokee Against Cherokee

Before the Trail of Tears, two groups of Cherokee had already settled in Indian Territory. The Old Settlers had traveled west decades ago, before the Cherokee's removal began. Members of the Treaty Party had come to Indian Territory later following the signing of the Treaty of New Echota in 1835.

The Cherokee who traveled on the Trail of Tears greatly outnumbered the other groups in the new Cherokee Nation. The newcomers wanted to reestablish their old government with John Ross as principal chief. The Old Settlers and the Treaty Party, though, were uncomfortable with this idea. The Treaty Party was especially unwilling to accept John Ross as the tribal leader. Because of their disagreements with Ross over removal, they considered him a political enemy.

The Treaty Party was right to worry. On June 22, 1839, Cherokee **vigilantes** attacked several Treaty Party leaders. They killed Elias Boudinot, Major Ridge, and his son John Ridge. Stand Watie, Boudinot's brother, was also marked for murder, but he was able to escape.

After the killings, the Cherokee seemed destined for civil war. To avoid that disaster, several Cherokee leaders met in September and drafted the Constitution of 1839. Similar to the constitution the Cherokee wrote in 1827, it named Ross as the tribe's leader.

Fighting between Cherokee groups continued, however. Seven years later, Ross, Watie, and other leaders finally agreed to make peace by signing the Treaty of 1846. Once they stopped battling one another, these leaders were finally able to start rebuilding the Cherokee Nation in the West.

Prospering in Indian Territory

Within only a few years, the tribe made great progress. It began publishing a new newspaper, the *Cherokee Advocate*. The tribe built schools to educate the Cherokee's children. By the end of the 1840s, the Cherokee school system included 144 elementary schools. The tribe also operated two seminaries, which were among the best schools for higher education in the region.

The Cherokee built many schools to provide education for their children.

Cherokee families worked hard to build new houses and farms. Many people became successful farmers and ranchers. A few became wealthy. As in the East, the wealthiest Cherokee lived in mansions and established large farms worked by African-American slaves.

Just as the Cherokee were getting on their feet, they were drawn into still another war. This conflict was the American Civil War (1861–1865). It pitted Americans in the northern states against Americans in the southern states. Those in the South wanted to break away from the United States. They formed their own country—the Confederate States of America, also called the Confederacy.

Most Cherokee did not want to get involved in the Americans' war. A few, though, wanted to side with the South. Many were slave owners. They knew that the North (also known as the Union) would outlaw slavery if it won the war.

Confederate officials pressured the tribe to become allies. John Ross tried to keep the Cherokee neutral, but the pro-South Cherokee were determined to fight. Ross feared that if the tribe did not join the Confederacy, the pro-South and the pro-North Cherokee would start fighting each other. Reluctantly, he signed a treaty with the Confederacy in August 1861.

The Civil War

Because of Ross's choice, the Cherokee became the enemy of the Union army. In the summer of 1862, the Union army invaded the Cherokee Nation. John Ross fled to Washington, D.C., where he spent the remainder of the war. In Ross's absence, Stand Watie named himself principal chief. A strong supporter of the South, Watie was a brigadier general in the Confederate army.

When the war ended in 1865, the Cherokee found themselves on the losing side. Even though many Cherokee had wanted to stay out of the war, the United States punished all of the Cherokee for being Confederate allies. The conditions of the tribe's 1866 peace treaty with the U.S. government were harsh. The Cherokee had to give up a great deal of land. Even worse, the war took a significant toll on the Cherokee population. About one-third of the Western Cherokee died during the fighting.

As they had after the Trail of Tears, the Western Cherokee once again set about rebuilding their nation. At the same time, they had to deal with the many non-Indians who were coming to their lands. In the late 1800s, railroads brought many Americans west. Soon,

Stand Watie became the principal chief of the Western Cherokee during the Civil War.

The Last General

Cherokee leader Stand Watie was the last Confederate general to surrender at the end of the Civil War.

they were clamoring for control over Cherokee lands in Indian Territory.

The U.S. government responded with the Act of 1893. This law divided the Cherokee Nation into small plots called **allotments**. Each qualified Cherokee was assigned an allotment. Non-Indians were then allowed to settle on the land that was left over.

In 1907, what had been the Cherokee Nation became part of the new state of Oklahoma. With statehood, the Cherokee government was disbanded. The tribe still had a principal chief but this leader was chosen not by the Cherokee, but by the president of the United States. The proud Cherokee of the West were no longer an independent people.

This photograph shows a Western Cherokee woman in the 1930s, which was a very difficult time for both the Western and Eastern Cherokee.

Chapter Six

The Modern Cherokee

In the early 1900s, survival was still a struggle for both the Eastern and the Western Cherokee. They were hit especially hard by the Great Depression of the 1930s. Like many people in the United States, they had trouble finding jobs during this period. In Oklahoma, a drought made the situation worse. As farms shut down, about one-third of the Western Cherokee had to leave the region and search for work elsewhere.

The Eastern Cherokee had some relief from the economic hard times after the opening of the Great Smoky Mountains National Park in 1934. The park was located near their lands in North Carolina. Soon, each year, many thousands of tourists were flocking to the region and spending money at tribal businesses.

The Cherokee Population

In the 2000 census, about 730,000 Americans identified themselves as Cherokee.

The Eastern Band of the Cherokee

The Eastern Cherokee established the Cherokee Historical Association in 1948. This organization took advantage of the tourist trade by sponsoring *Unto These Hills*, a drama that tells the history of the Cherokee up to the Trail of Tears. Since its debut in 1950, the play has been performed every summer. It has been seen by more than five million people.

In the 1950s, the Eastern Cherokee also established Oconaluftee Indian Village. The attraction features a recreation of an eighteenth-century Cherokee village. Visitors can also watch Cherokee artists create pottery, masks, and other crafts. Traditional arts are also kept alive by the Qualla Arts and Crafts Mutual. This successful cooperative sells the work of contemporary Cherokee artists and operates a gallery.

Recently, the Eastern Cherokee opened a casino in western North Carolina. This enterprise helps fund programs admin-

The Qualla Boundary

The Eastern Cherokee hold about 56,000 acres in western North Carolina. These lands are known as the Qualla Boundary.

An Eastern Cherokee woman beads a belt. She is one of the many craftspeople who work at the Oconaluftee Indian Village.

istered by the band's government. This government is led by a principal chief and a twelve-member tribal council. These representatives are chosen through election by the almost 10,000 people on the band's official rolls.

The Cherokee Nation of Oklahoma

Like their eastern kin, the Western Cherokee have prospered in recent decades. About 220,000 people are official members of the Cherokee Nation of Oklahoma. Today, Western Cherokee are found all over the world, though many live in the fourteen counties in the northeastern corner of the state.

The Western Cherokee reorganized their government in the 1970s. They began electing their principal chiefs in 1971 and wrote a new constitution in 1975. From its headquarters

Wilma Mankiller

In 1987, the Oklahoma Cherokee elected Wilma Mankiller principal chief, making her the first woman to lead a major Native American tribe.

The Cherokee Heritage Center offers visitors many ways to learn about Cherokee culture and history.

in Tahlequah, the Cherokee Nation tribal council operates a wide variety of programs to provide job training, health care, education, and quality housing for tribe members.

Many of these programs are funded by tribal businesses. These include two convenience stores, a gift shop, and three casinos. The tribe also operates Cherokee Nation Industries, which has several manufacturing contracts with U.S. Department of Defense.

To preserve Cherokee history and culture, the tribe established the Cherokee Heritage Center in Park Hill, Oklahoma.

The United Keetoowah Band

In 1950, the United States formally recognized a third branch of the Cherokee—the United Keetoowah Band. The Keetoowah people trace their roots to the Cherokee traditionalists who voluntarily left their homeland for western lands in the early nineteenth century. With a population of more than seven thousand, the Keetoowah believe they are the true Cherokee tribe.

The complex includes a 1,500-seat amphitheater, a re-creation of an ancient Cherokee village, and the Cherokee National Museum. On May 12, 2001, the museum unveiled a permanent exhibit on the Trail of Tears. One of the most popular features of the exhibit is the Memorial Bead Wall. The 28-foot (8.5-m) wall is woven from 16,000 handmade beads—one for each Cherokee who marched west along the trail.

An eternal flame burns in Red Clay State Park in Red Clay, Tennessee, in honor of the Cherokee people.

Into the Future

Since the 1830s, the Western and Eastern Cherokee have been separated by hundreds of miles. Nevertheless, they have remained closely tied by their shared history and culture. Recognizing their bonds, representatives from each group came together in Red Clay, Tennessee, in 1984 for their first joint tribal council. Since that historic event, a council has met at Red Clay every two years to discuss issues of importance to all Cherokee people.

The Cherokee of the West and of the East are also united by their pride in being the Ani-Yun-Wiya—the principal people. Despite centuries of war, disease, and poverty, they have remained strong. Knowing what their ancestors were able to overcome, the Cherokee of today are confident in their ability not only to survive but also to prosper.

Timeline

1540	Spaniards led by Hernando de Soto encounter Indians of the Southeast.
1760	Cherokee territory is invaded by the English during the French and Indian War.
1785	Cherokee negotiate the Treaty of Hopewell with the United States.
1802	United States promises Georgia to end Cherokee landownership in the state.
1819	A group of Cherokee traditionalists chooses to leave the tribal lands and become U.S. citizens.
1827	Cherokee leaders write the tribe's first constitution.
1828	The *Cherokee Phoenix* begins publication.
1829	Gold is discovered in Cherokee territory.
1830	Congress passes the Indian Removal Act, calling for the relocation of the Cherokee and other eastern tribes to Indian Territory.
1832	U.S. Supreme Court protects the Cherokee's right to govern themselves in its ruling in *Worcester v. Georgia*.
1835	A minority of the Cherokee leaders sign the Treaty of New Echota, which calls for the tribe's removal.
1838–1839	Thousands of Cherokee march to Indian Territory on the Trail of Tears.

1839	Cherokee leaders are assassinated for signing the Treaty of New Echota in June. The Cherokee of Indian Territory adopt a new constitution in September.
1861	Principal Chief John Ross allies the Western Cherokee to the Confederacy during the American Civil War.
1866	Cherokee in Indian Territory negotiate a peace treaty with the United States.
1893	The Act of 1893 calls for the allotment of the lands of the Western Cherokee.
1907	The Cherokee Nation in the West becomes part of Oklahoma.
1934	The Great Smoky Mountains National Park opens near the Eastern Cherokee's lands.
1948	The Eastern Cherokee establish the Cherokee Historical Association.
1950	The United Keetoowah Band of Cherokee is formally recognized by the the United States. The Eastern Cherokee debut *Unto These Hills*.
1975	The Western Cherokee write a constitution, establishing a new tribal government.
1984	Representatives of the Eastern and Western Cherokee attend a joint tribal council in Red Clay, Tennessee.
2001	The Cherokee National Museum unveils a permanent exhibit on the Trail of Tears.

Glossary

allotment—a plot of land assigned to an individual Indian as privately owned property

Ani-Yun-Wiya—the name (meaning "principal people") the Cherokee traditionally called themselves

black drink—a tea drunk by the Cherokee to purify their bodies

clan—a group of relatives within a tribe

Green Corn Ceremony—a ceremony performed each summer by the Cherokee to celebrate the ripening of the corn crop

immunity—a naturally produced substance that helps bodies fight disease-causing germs

Indian Territory—an area in what is now Oklahoma to which most Cherokee were forced to relocate in the 1830s

missionary—a person who tries to convert others to their religion

principal chief—a title given to the leader of the Cherokee beginning in the early nineteenth century

removal—the nineteenth-century U.S. policy of relocating eastern Indians to lands west of the Mississippi River

traditionalist—a tribe member who retained traditional customs and rejected non-Indian ways

Trail of Tears—the journey taken by about 16,000 Cherokee from their southeastern homeland to Indian Territory in the late 1830s

treaty—a formal agreement between two nations

Treaty Party—a group of Cherokee who negotiated the 1835 Treaty of New Echota that called for the tribe's relocation to Indian Territory

vigilante—a person who works outside the law to punish alleged wrongdoers

war women—respected Cherokee women who accompanied the tribe's warriors into battle

To Find Out More

Books

Bealer, Alex W. *Only the Names Remain: The Cherokees and the Trail of Tears*. Boston: Little, Brown & Co., 1996.

Bruchac, Joseph. *The Journal of Jessie Smoke: A Cherokee Boy*. New York: Scholastic, 2001.

Hoig, Stanley. *Night of the Cruel Moon: Cherokee Removal and the Trail of Tears*. New York: Facts on File, 1996.

Klausner, Janet. *Sequoyah's Gift: A Portrait of the Cherokee Leader*. New York: HarperCollins, 1993.

Perdue, Theda. *The Cherokee*. New York: Chelsea House
    Publishers, 1989.

Roop, Peter, and Connie Roop. *If You Lived with the Cherokee*.
    New York: Scholastic, 1998.

Organizations and Online Sites

All Things Cherokee
http://www.allthingscherokee.com
This helpful site offers articles about Cherokee history, language, and culture, as well as many links to related web sources.

The Cherokee Nation of Oklahoma
http://www.cherokee.org
This official site of the Western Cherokee features news about contemporary events and back issues of *Cherokee Phoenix* newspaper.

The Eastern Band of the Cherokee Indians
http://www.cherokee-nc.com
Intended primarily for tourists, the Eastern Cherokee's site provides information for visitors to their lands and descriptions of tribally operated attractions.

A Note on Sources

The history and culture of the Cherokee have been widely documented. A good starting point in studying the tribe is Theda Perdue's *The Cherokee*. Although its language and perspective are somewhat dated, *The Cherokees* by Grace Steele Woodward is also a solid general survey of Cherokee history.

For the Trail of Tears era, I've relied on Stan Hoig's brief but well-researched *Night of the Cruel Moon*. The highly readable *Trail of Tears: The Rise and Fall of the Cherokee Nation* by John Ehle is also useful. An excellent source on the Western Cherokee during the post-removal period is William G. McLoughlin's *After the Trail of Tears: The Cherokee's Struggle for Sovereignty*. Also essential is John Finger's *The Eastern Band of the Cherokee*. For contemporary issues, the Web site of the Cherokee Nation of Oklahoma is a particularly useful source.

—Liz Sonneborn

Index

Numbers in *italics* indicate illustrations.

About the Author

Liz Sonneborn is a writer and an editor who lives in Brooklyn, New York. A graduate of Swarthmore College, she specializes in books about the history and culture of American Indians as well as the biographies of noteworthy people in American history. She has written more than thirty books for children and adults, including *A to Z of Native American Women* and *The New York Public Library's Amazing Native American History*, winner of a Parents' Choice Award.